Prayer Guide

Growing a Christ-centered Life

Stella Ma

2nd Edition (2018)

ISBN-10: 1537100238
ISBN-13: 978-1537100234
(Paperback)

Dedication

To my grandmother,
who modeled a life of prayer,
service and godly devotion.

Author's Note

No publication is possible without community support and expertise. I am thankful to all my friends, family, ministry communities, and prayer partners. Their encouragement, prayers, and support have made this resource possible.

This prayer guide was inspired by my years of spiritual formation ministry among leaders, missionaries and churches. I am grateful to my community, *Imago Christi*, CRM. Their lives and ministry have enabled me to discover a deeper spiritual life, one anchored in Christ through prayer.

My heartfelt thanks to Dr. June Hetzel for her loving support, and editing partnership over the years. My thanks also to Bill O'Byrne and Ralph Dawson for their assistance and support in bringing this book to fruition.

Contents

Preface

This prayer guide grew out of two desires. The first was a longing to live a life more fully centered on Christ, one characterized by unhurried listening and loving obedience. This desire led to my pursuit of an intentional life of spiritual rhythms, beginning with the foundation of daily prayer.

The second desire was to provide a resource to others who share this longing to live more anchored in Christ. This prayer resource is for other believers and leaders, who wish to cooperate with God's transforming work in life and ministry. In particular, it offers a concrete response to those who ask, "Given my circumstances, how do I live a life more centered on Christ?"

So let us consider the possibility of "kingdom life" in the present, through a framework or "trellis," a way of life anchored in Christ, nourished by a robust love of God, rather than one ruled by dictates of work and culture, as important as they are.

Many are experiencing an awakening, a sense that God is inviting His loved ones to a deeper walk with Him. How then can we respond to God's invitation? How may we make a meaningful change?

This invitation draws individuals, like myself, to seek a more "rooted" prayer life, building on the prayer rudiments of petitions, praise and confession. Yet any consistency in spiritual practices, specifically prayer, is challenging in the wake of many demands and a fast-paced life, the reality of many. Perhaps we can begin by making a fresh, intentional effort at a prayer-filled life.

Prayer is primarily a relating to God, thus building a prayer life is about creating a substantial place to be with God. The gift of growing a prayer life is that it enables us to weave several spiritual disciplines including scripture, meditation, confession, and silence, into one cohesive and sustainable pattern in our daily routines. One form of prayer practice is the recitation of "daily offices," a structured approach I have found helpful, one that is familiar at some level to many Christians from different traditions.

This prayer guide intends to refresh and revive the practice of daily offices across denominations and cultures, for those who, like myself, wish to live with more awareness of God's presence and grace in the daily.

Many Protestant churches will have experienced aspects of the offices through their personal prayers and corporate worship. Many in liturgical traditions who use prayer guides already use daily offices.

With this prayer guide, you are invited to pause daily, whether morning, noon, evening, or whenever your schedule allows. Whether at work or at home, you can choose to enter a quiet, inner sanctum, to be in God's presence.

If you are seeking help in your walk with Christ, especially your prayer life, this guide maybe a good place to begin. Perhaps you are in transition or travel for work like I do. A simple rhythm of a morning and evening office may help anchor you, in an environment of constant change. Whether you find yourself mired spiritually or yearning to explore uncharted waters of spiritual living, this invitation is for you.

1

Why use a Prayer Guide?

God is calling us into a deeper relationship with Him. Our relationship with God is forged in the soil of the ordinary. Consistent prayer, our communion with the Trinitarian God, is both root and fruit of an abundant life in Christ.

The Lord Christ, our Teacher, showed us what it means to live a life in constant communion with God. The Holy Spirit, our Guide and Intercessor, draws us into a deeper relationship with the Father, Creator of all life and Giver of all good gifts.

Our prayer routines form a dynamic prayer life that may change as we mature in Christ. We learn how to pray from others who are more mature or experienced, hence the need for resources, models and guides.

Just as a child-parent relationship shifts from the level of communicating needs, what I might consider one dimensional, to more listening and non-verbal communication, one that is multi-dimensional, as part of maturity, so our prayer practice may also reflect this pattern. Incorporating a daily rhythm of prayers is one aspect of prayer growth.

Our personal prayer life as beginners may include memorizing the Lord's (Disciples') Prayer, and asking for our needs. As we mature, we learn to build on basics, praying more deeply with Scriptures and the Psalms, interceding for others, leaning into confession, adoration, thanksgiving, and perhaps, embracing more silence.

How do we live a life centered on Christ?

The habit of pausing for prayer throughout the day, the rhythm and frequency which a daily office encourages, nurtures our longing for God. While a brief daily prayer or bible study is helpful, observing pauses for the Word and worship throughout the day as a routine will help increase our inner "room" for God; His presence, instruction, insights, and blessings.

This is the primary intent of a daily office–creating a quiet space, the turning of heart, mind, body and soul towards Christ in the flow of the day, so that we may orient our heart and choices more and more around Christ's heart and presence.

While a framework for a thriving spiritual life requires more than a daily structure of personal worship, a Christ-centered life cannot be sustained without unhurried, regular communion with God. Thus we find balance in shifting change, refreshment in midst of our many tasks, and direction for daily life.

This spiritual practice frames a rhythm of ongoing connection with God, a way of abiding in Christ and noticing the movement of the Holy Spirit in and through us. This one prayer form encompasses many spiritual practices and weaves them into a simple, elegant pattern.

How do we live now as God's people?

In every age, followers of Christ are faced with the challenge of living with, and within the holy presence of God. Regular worship including prayer is contextualized and embraced in every generation, within the milieu of evolving lifestyles, culture and history.

Spiritual rhythms like prayer characterize God's people. In the Body of Christ, daily practices of key spiritual disciplines, such as Scripture meditation, silence and prayer evident in the daily offices, have been persistently observed and taught by the apostles and leaders of the early Church. These practices proclaim and usher in the unseen realities of the spiritual realm and the greater truth of God's Kingdom.

Therefore, these spiritual rhythms are a vital part of our legacy and a source of present and future blessing. We can only authentically offer that which we have experienced, and by which we have been transformed. This means that it is our responsibility to preserve the legacy passed on to us by first establishing the practices in our lives. Then and thus modeling it to our families, communities, new believers and the future generations.

There are several listings and descriptions of spiritual practices available to us today. Whatever range and form of spiritual practices we may choose to identify and use, the intentional engagement of body, mind and spirit in the prayer and worship of God, beyond Sunday observances and occasional meditation and devotional times, are essential to spiritual transformation. God uses them to transform us into the image of the Christ.

We may have the priorities in reverse. Our personal communion with God leads to sustainable and effective ministry. Our Lord Christ models this communion out of which ministry flows. The reverse is often practiced and in the long run, unsustainable and even unhealthy.

Some have expressed concerns that spiritual disciplines may create an unhealthy inward focus that distracts us from our mission to reach the world for Christ. Paradoxically, these spiritual practices actually serve our ministry calling. They enable us to be more engaged in other communities. Growth in our personal prayer life generates both desire and ability to live a life more intentionally focused on God's will, as well as engage in the Holy Spirit's work in the world.

Often relational, work, and ministerial demands drown or suffocate what God intends to accomplish in us. When we are limited in our understanding, experience, and intentionality, we may miss the opportunity, the divine invitation, to grow deeper in our communion with God, who is Life and Love.

This invitation requires our cooperation. When we choose to make room, to slow down and take time to wait on God, we allow Him to work in us, and for us, in ways we may not fully comprehend.

A reminder: practices like prayer are not about earning God's favor. Nor do the use of them make us more righteous. Through Christ we already have God's favor and our righteousness is already secured by His blood. Spiritual practices are means to an end and not an end in themselves. They enable us to cooperate with God's transforming and sanctifying work in us. They may trip us up if we lose sight of why we are using them.

2

What is a Daily Office?

Daily offices form a creative, yet time-honored way for the follower of Christ, or communities of disciples, to make space for God in their full and complex lives. They provide a framework for daily worship of God, a way of encountering and living out the normal, within the sphere of the Divine Trinity.

Offices are observed in several Christian traditions, and are varied in their number, composition, and duration. In some Christian traditions, a daily office is also called a divine service. The term "office" comes from the Latin word *"officium"* or translated as "duty" expressing the Christian responsibility and privilege to pray, not only on Sundays, but daily praying with the Church.

In historical and current practice, daily offices comprise a cycle of daily worship times, refreshing pauses throughout a day. Depending on the community involved, these may range from one to seven in number, and serve as extensions of a daily time of meditation, a practice familiar to many Christians.

Many believe that this prayer practice has its roots in Jewish worship and the early church. Daily prayer observances may be found in the New Testament. For example, we read that the apostles, Peter and John, went to the Temple to pray at noon (Acts 3:1). This rhythm of prayer developed into this structured form during the monastic movement, which saw a flourishing of structured spiritual practices.

How do we use this framework?

Three offices or mini-services are offered each day of the week, and may be used by an individual or a group. For those who wish to begin with one service each day, there are offices sufficient for twenty-one days. For those who observe all three daily, the morning, afternoon and evening offices, a cycle of seven days is provided. The same cycle may be repeated for the next week as long as desired.

These offices are intended to be read aloud, unlike the more customary silent reading of devotional material and Scriptures. Verbalizing allows us to move beyond mental engagement to greater body, heart, and spirit participation. A truth spoken also has a better chance to take root in the memory and thence the heart.

Repetition is a "friend" to our spiritual growth. Repetition fosters an inward anchored-ness that is in fact essential. Each office or mini-worship time includes a balance of rich silence and spoken responses.

A responsive format has been provided to enable community prayer or group worship times. The italicized lettering indicates participation or response when used in a group setting. The facilitator reads the sections in between italicized responses.

For simplicity of use, for the less experienced in liturgical or structured worship, I have made a selection of common essentials from other traditional worship guides.

What are the main parts of this "daily office"?

Affirmation

We begin to place a theme in our hearts and minds for the day. The first opening words usually affirm God's sovereignty and handiwork in our lives and the world around us. This focus enables us to open ourselves to the unseen, greater reality of God's Kingdom, and God's substantial movement. We proclaim aloud what we believe, engaging not only our minds but also all of our being.

Silence

In silence we acknowledge and welcome God into our day. Allow a long pause of a few minutes. As we learn to be still with God, we relinquish our need for sound and embrace silence as a unique gift. This time of silence is not at all passive. We are learning to shed distractions, gathering our hearts and minds, to focus entirely on God. This silence is less about letting go of the outer hearing sensation, and more about creating an uncluttered, inner space to attend to God who is Mystery. This silence is not only a clearing out of distraction, but a space for more of God. The silent space we enter within is full of God's presence.

Acclamation or Response

These are opportunities to connect with the theme of the day, and to deepen our awareness of the Lord's presence with us, and His activity for and in us. Our "Response" acknowledges that we are part of a sacred community of believers, grafted in Christ, beyond our current location and reality.

Scripture Reading

Selections are generally short, primarily to encourage memorization over time. Usually portions from Psalms, plus a "Little Chapter," or passages from the Gospels, New and/ or Old Testaments are read. In some Christian traditions, the Psalms are read on a continuous cycle so that all one hundred and fifty psalms are covered at least once in the course of the year. The chosen psalm may be read responsively in a group, with facilitator and group reading alternate verses.

Canticles

These are "acts of prayer and praise"* based on Scripture. It may be a hymn or a praise song. From Latin *"canticulum"* which means "little song." Worship is an aspect central to an office. We are ushered into the presence of God and the heavenlies when we participate in this God-given task.

Worship not only declares God's truth and glory as God commanded, but it also serves as a channel by which we are transformed. We are thus recipients on more than one dimension.

Worship, as a spiritual discipline, flows back to us as a source of blessings. We may not always be aware, but we are empowered, enlivened, often transformed as the breath and life of God, which we proclaim, flows back through the Holy Spirit.

Prayers

    The canticle may be followed by one or more of three prayer forms: prayers of confession, a time of intercession, or corporate prayer such as a reading of the Apostle's Creed. This creed and other selections may be found in the later chapter on "Other Helps."

1. Confession
This practice enables us to keep a short list of our weaknesses and sins. Forgiveness asked and extended is important to nurture Christian virtues like humility, in tandem with vanquishing our vices, especially pride. The Latin prayer *"Kyrie eleison"* or *"Lord have mercy"* is a traditional prayer of confession and contrition.

2. Intercession
These may be a written prayer read, or spontaneously offered around a word or theme. For example, simply naming aloud individuals we know who have a specific need, such as healing or encouragement.

3. Corporate Prayer and Response
Traditional prayers like the Lord's (Disciples') Prayer, Psalm 23, the Doxology, and the *"Gloria Patri"*** are integral elements of the offices. Declarative responses such as the Apostle's or Nicene creeds are also recommended.

    Consider the Lord's Prayer. This simple yet profound prayer covers the length, breadth, and depth of our lives. It both integrates and concludes our confession and intercession time. To pray in the timeless words as Christ taught His disciples invites us to move beyond our private experience to the spiritual realities of the legacy of our faith, the eternal community we share with the faithful generations who have gone before, and those who now live and those who will come after us.

Collect

This section includes prayers or choruses sung. They simply assist us in collecting our thoughts thus far, an opportunity to offer a praise response to the Lord.

Affirmation

We acknowledge once more the theme of the day. The closing affirmation also reminds us of whom God is to us, beyond what He does. This voices the basis of our identity in Christ, the foundation on which all our activity rests. We speak and affirm our desire to carry this awareness of our identity in Christ into the new day.

Benediction

We acknowledge our dependence on a loving and generous God, ending the office by speaking or sharing a blessing, a gift of unmerited grace.

A note of encouragement as you continue. Prayer is a labor of loving God and experiencing His love for us, but it is nonetheless soul labor. This prayer practice will take patience, effort, trust, and surrender. This is not a quick remedy for a spiritual malaise.

A prayer rhythm is not intended to be burdensome but really to 'lighten' our inner load by teaching us to rely on God and the resources He provides. It may not seem so at first, but the beginning effort will give way to greater ease with practice. So be gentle with yourself.

The pursuit of God is a journey of faith, fraught with challenge and struggle. Prayer is no exception. Results or rewards may take time. However, in the fray of the struggle, there will be deeper blessings of God's love, grace, blessing and growth.

May the Trinity, Father, Son and Spirit, hold, strengthen, and inspire you as you explore undiscovered spiritual landscapes and deepen your life in Christ.

3

A Daily Rhythm of Prayer

Sunday - *Trinity*

Monday - *Resting*

Tuesday - *God Almighty*

Wednesday - *Longing*

Thursday - *Jesus Christ*

Friday - *Abiding*

Saturday - *Holy Spirit*

Sunday

Trinity

Morning – Trinity ✶

Arise! O my soul
Rejoice with heart and voice.
Lift your heart, body and mind.
Alleluia!

Silence

†Arise! O Bride of Christ,
Enter in with thankfulness
The earthly chorus and heavenly song
Exult and adore our King.

Past to present, east to west
Guided by the Spirit,
Under the blood of the Lamb.
Alleluia!

Psalm 100 (KJV)

Make a joyful noise unto the Lord, all ye lands.
Serve the Lord with gladness:
Come before His presence with singing.

Know ye that the Lord He is God:
It is He that hath made us, and not we ourselves;
We are His people, and the sheep of His pasture.

Enter into His gates with thanksgiving,
And into His courts with praise:
Be thankful unto Him, and bless His name.
For the Lord is good; His mercy is everlasting;
And His truth endureth to all generations.

---

† For groups, *italicized* words are corporately spoken or sung responses.

Genesis 1: 1-3, 5, 26-28, 31 (NASB)

In the beginning God created the heavens and the earth.
The earth was formless and void,
and darkness was over the surface of the deep,
and the Spirit of God was moving over the surface of the waters.
Then God said, "Let there be light"; and there was light.
...And there was evening and there was morning, one day.

Then God said, "Let Us make man in Our image,
according to Our likeness;
and let them rule over the fish of the sea,
and over the birds of the sky and
over the cattle and over all the earth,
and over every creeping thing that creeps on the earth."
God created man in His own image,
in the image of God He created him;
male and female He created them.

God blessed them..."Be fruitful and multiply,
and fill the earth and subdue it;
and rule over the fish of the sea and over the birds of the sky
and over every living thing that moves on the earth."

God saw all that He had made,
and behold, it was very good.
And there was evening and there was morning, the sixth day.

†Hymn: Joyful, Joyful, We Adore Thee

1. Joyful, joyful, we adore Thee,
God of glory, Lord of love;
Hearts unfold like flow'rs before Thee,
Op'ning to the sun above.
Melt the clouds of sin and sadness;
Drive the dark of doubt away;

---

† For groups, *italicized* words are corporately spoken or sung responses.

Giver of immortal gladness,
Fill us with the light of day!

2. All Thy works with joy surround Thee,
Earth and heav'n reflect Thy rays,
Stars and angels sing around Thee,
Center of unbroken praise.
Field and forest, vale and mountain,
Flow'ry meadow, flashing sea,
Singing bird and flowing fountain
Call us to rejoice in Thee.

Silence

Our Father who art in Heaven
Hallowed be Thy Name
Thy Kingdom come,
Thy will be done on earth
As it is in Heaven.

Give us this day our daily bread
And forgive us our trespasses
As we forgive those that trespass against us.
Lead us not into temptation
But deliver us from evil,
For Thine is the Kingdom
And the power and glory and honour,
Forever and ever. Amen.

We pray for our brothers and sisters.
Those who are hungry and needy.
(Pause for silent intercession.)

Those who are sick and dying.
(Pause to pray silently.)

Those who have strayed from Thy presence.
(Pause to pray silently.)

Those who are living and working in difficult situations.
(Pause to pray silently.)

Restore the broken bodies and spirits.
Lord, prepare us for your Kingdom.

Rescue the lost and afflicted ones.
Lord, prepare us for your Kingdom.

Strengthen the weary and discouraged.
Lord, prepare us for your Kingdom.

The grace of the Lord Jesus Christ, and the love of God,
And the communion of the Holy Spirit be with you all.
Amen.*

Afternoon – Trinity 🕊

Bless the Lord,
O my soul,
Declare His glorious works,
Now and evermore.

Silence

†*Praise God from whom all blessings flow*
Praise Him all creatures here below
Praise Him above ye heavenly hosts
Praise Father, Son and Holy Ghost.
Amen.

<u>Psalm 150 (NKJV)</u>

Praise the Lord!
Praise God in His sanctuary;
Praise Him in His mighty firmament!
Praise Him for His mighty acts;
Praise Him according to His excellent greatness!
Praise Him with the sound of the trumpet;
Praise Him with the lute and harp!
Praise Him with the timbrel and dance;
Praise Him with stringed instruments and flutes!
Praise Him with loud cymbals;
Praise Him with clashing cymbals!
Let everything that has breath praise the Lord.
Praise the Lord!

<u>Hymn: Joyful, Joyful, We Adore Thee</u>

1. Thou art giving and forgiving,
Ever blessing, ever blest,

---

† For groups, *italicized* words are corporately spoken or sung responses.

18

Wellspring of the joy of living,
Ocean depth of happy rest!
Thou our Father, Christ our Brother,
All who live in love are Thine;
Teach us how to love each other,
Lift us to the joy divine.

2. *Mortals, join the happy chorus,*
Which the morning stars began;
Father love is reigning o'er us,
Brother love binds man to man.
Ever singing, march we onward,
Victors in the midst of strife,
Joyful music leads us Sunward
In the triumph song of life.

Silence

May the grace of Christ our Savior
And the Father's boundless love
With the Holy Spirit's favor,
Rest upon us from above.

Thus may we abide in union
With each other and the Lord,
And possess, in sweet communion,
Joys which earth cannot afford.**

The grace of the Lord Jesus Christ, and the love of God,
And the communion of the Holy Spirit be with you all.
Amen.

Evening – Trinity 🎶

Bless the Lord and give thanks.
Eternity dwells within us.
The Kingdom of God is at hand.
Alleluia!

Silence

†How great art Thou, O Lord Almighty.
Heaven and earth declare Thy glory.
O people of God
Dance and sing,
Leap and shout,
How great art Thou, O Lord Almighty.

Revelation 21: 1-7; 9-11; 21-23 (NKJV)

Now I saw a new heaven and a new earth,
for the first heaven and the first earth had passed away...
Then I, John, saw the holy city, New Jerusalem,
coming down out of heaven from God,
prepared as a bride adorned for her husband.

And I heard a loud voice from heaven saying,
"Behold, the tabernacle of God is with men,
and He will dwell with them, and they shall be His people.
God Himself will be with them and be their God.

And God will wipe away every tear from their eyes;
there shall be no more death, nor sorrow...no more pain,
for the former things have passed away.
...Behold, I make all things new.

---

† For groups, *italicized* words are corporately spoken or sung responses.

...I am the Alpha and the Omega, the Beginning and the End.
I will give of the fountain of the water of life
freely to him who thirsts.
He who overcomes shall inherit all things,
and I will be his God and he shall be My son."

Then one of the seven angels...came and talked with me, saying,
"Come, I will show you the bride, the Lamb's wife."
And he carried me away in the Spirit to a great and high mountain,
and showed me the great city, the holy Jerusalem,
descending out of heaven from God, having the glory of God.

Her light was like a most precious stone...clear as crystal.
The twelve gates were twelve pearls...
And the street of the city was pure gold, like transparent glass.

But I saw no temple in it,
for the Lord God Almighty and the Lamb are its temple.
The city had no need of the sun or of the moon to shine in it,
for the glory of God illuminated it.
The Lamb is its light.

†*Hymn: Holy, Holy, Holy*

1. *Holy, holy, holy! Lord God Almighty!*
Early in the morning our song shall rise to Thee.
Holy, holy, holy! Merciful and mighty,
God in three Persons, blessed Trinity!

2. *Holy, holy, holy! All the saints adore Thee,*
Casting down their golden crowns around the glassy sea;
Cherubim and seraphim falling down before Thee,
Which wert, and art, and evermore shalt be.

3. *Holy, holy, holy! Lord God Almighty!*
All Thy works shall praise Thy name, in earth and sky and sea.

---

† For groups, *italicized* words are corporately spoken or sung responses.

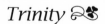

Holy, holy, holy! Merciful and mighty,
God in three Persons, blessed Trinity.

Silence

Our Father who art in Heaven
Hallowed be Thy Name
Thy Kingdom come,
Thy will be done on earth
As it is in Heaven.

Give us this day our daily bread
And forgive us our trespasses
As we forgive those that trespass against us.
Lead us not into temptation
But deliver us from evil,

For Thine is the Kingdom
And the power and glory and honour,
Forever and ever. Amen

Maranatha. Lord come quickly.

Glories too bright to behold,
Blessings too brimming to grasp,
Love incomprehensible.
Yet such is our legacy,
Such is our growing reality.

Maranatha. Lord come quickly.

Silence

The grace of the Lord Jesus Christ, and the love of God,
And the communion of the Holy Spirit be with you all.
Amen.

Trinity 🙢

Monday

Resting

Morning – Resting ❧

Come now beloved of the Lord,
Be still and rest in God.

Silence

Lord, lead us to Your pastures
We pause to listen and receive.

Lord, we come just as we are.
Open us, heart, body, and mind
To Your invitation and gift today.

<u>*Psalm 37: 3-11 (NKJV)*</u>

Trust in the Lord, and do good...
Delight yourself also in the Lord,
and He shall give you the desires of your heart.
Commit your way to the Lord...
and He shall bring it to pass.
He shall bring forth your righteousness as the light...

Rest in the Lord, and wait patiently for Him;
do not fret because of him who prospers in his way,
because of the man who brings wicked schemes to pass.
Cease from anger, and forsake wrath...
For evildoers shall be cut off;
But those who wait on the Lord, they shall inherit the earth.

For yet a little while and the wicked shall be no more...
But the meek shall inherit the earth,
and shall delight themselves in the abundance of peace.

I Kings 19: 1-8 (NKJV)

And Ahab told Jezebel all that Elijah had done,
also how he had executed all the prophets with the sword.
Then Jezebel sent a messenger to Elijah, saying,
"So let the gods do to me, and more also, if I do not make your life
as the life of one of them by tomorrow about this time."

And when he saw that, he arose and ran for his life,
... a day's journey into the wilderness,
...And he prayed that he might die, and said,
"It is enough! Now, Lord, take my life,
for I am no better than my fathers!"

Then as he lay and slept under a broom tree,
suddenly an angel touched him,
and said to him, "Arise and eat."
Then he looked, and there by his head
was a cake baked on coals, and a jar of water.
So he ate and drank, and lay down again.

And the angel of the Lord came back the second time,
and touched him, and said,
"Arise and eat, because the journey is too great for you."
So he arose, and ate and drank;
and he went in the strength of that food
forty days and forty nights
as far as Horeb, the mountain of God.

Hymn: For the Beauty of the Earth

1. For the beauty of the earth
For the glory of the skies,
For the love which from our birth
Over and around us lies.

Refrain
Lord of all, to Thee we raise,
This our hymn of grateful praise.

2. For the beauty of each hour,
Of the day and of the night,
Hill and vale, and tree and flower,
Sun and moon, and stars of light.
Refrain

3. For the joy of ear and eye,
For the heart and mind's delight,
For the mystic harmony
Linking sense to sound and sight.
Refrain

Silence

Lord hear our petitions today.
(Pause for intercession)
(Name a need e.g., health, then name someone who comes to mind related to that need.)

The Lord is my shepherd;
I shall not want.
He makes me to lie down in green pastures;
He leads me beside the still waters.

He restores my soul;
He leads me in the paths of righteousness
For His name's sake.

Yea, though I walk through the valley of the shadow of death,
I will fear no evil;
For You are with me;

Your rod and Your staff,
They comfort me.
You prepare a table before me
In the presence of my enemies;

You anoint my head with oil;
My cup runs over.

Surely goodness and mercy shall follow me
All the days of my life;
And I will dwell
In the house of the Lord forever.*
Amen.

For all You provide today.
Thank you Lord,

For a long deep breath.
Thank you Lord,

For grace to slow our pace.
Thank you Lord,

You remove the hurdles around and within.
We come weary, worn, wounded,
Guide us with strong yet gentle Arms.
Alleluia.

Almighty God, open our minds to see
Your hand upon us.
Show us Your presence and provision
In our journeys past and present.

Give us sight to perceive You,
Diligence to seek You,
Patience to wait on You,
An attentive mind to dwell on You,
And a humble heart to receive of You.

In the name of the Father, Son and Holy Spirit.
Amen.

The Lord be with us this day and evermore.

Afternoon – Resting 〜

You Lord call us to work and to rest.
Give us strength in our work
And wisdom to rest in the midst of life.

Silence

Praise God from whom all blessings flow
Praise Him all creatures here below
Praise Him above ye heavenly hosts
Praise Father, Son and Holy Ghost.**
Amen.

Psalm 37: 6-7a (NKJV)

He shall bring forth your righteousness as the light,
and your justice as the noonday.
Rest in the Lord,
and wait patiently for Him;

Hymn: For the Beauty of the Earth

1. For the beauty of each hour,
Of the day and of the night,
Hill and vale, and tree and flower,
Sun and moon, and stars of light

Refrain
Lord of all, to Thee we raise,
This our hymn of grateful praise.

2. For the joy of human love,
Brother, sister, parent, child,
Friends on earth and friends above,
For all gentle thoughts and mild.
Refrain

Silence

A deep breath in both labor and rest
Thank you Lord for this,
A space to reflect on the morning.

Lord now we ask;
For peace in life's fray
Joy as we pause in stillness.

Moment by moment
May we live
More anchored in Your grace.

In the name of the Father, Son and Holy Spirit.
Amen.

The Lord be with us this day and evermore.

Evening – Resting 🐦

O chosen ones,
Citizens of God's Kingdom,
Be still and know that He is Lord.

Silence

Lord, lead us beside still waters.
We pause to hear Your voice.

Dear Lord, as we gather
At the close of this day
Seal in us Your words and insights,
Rest our hearts, mind and soul
Protect us through the night
Give us this night Your peace
Prepare us to return tomorrow.

Matthew 6:25-33 (NKJV)

Therefore I say to you, do not worry about your life,
what you will eat or what you will drink;
nor about your body, what you will put on...
Look at the birds of the air, for they neither sow nor reap...
yet your heavenly Father feeds them.

Are you not of more value than they?...
Consider the lilies of the field, how they grow:
they neither toil nor spin; and yet
I say to you that even Solomon in all his glory
was not arrayed like one of these...

Therefore do not worry, saying, 'What shall we eat?'
or 'What shall we drink?' or 'What shall we wear?'
For after all these things the Gentiles seek.
For your heavenly Father knows that you need all these things.

But seek first the kingdom of God and His righteousness,
and all these things shall be added to you.

<u>*Hymn: For the Beauty of the Earth*</u>

1. For Thy Church, that evermore
Lifteth holy hands above,
Offering up on every shore
Her pure sacrifice of love.

Refrain
Lord of all, to Thee we raise,
This our hymn of grateful praise.

2. For each perfect gift of Thine,
To our race so freely given,
Graces human and divine,
Flowers of earth and buds of Heaven.
Refrain

Silence

The Lord is my shepherd;
I shall not want.
He makes me to lie down in green pastures;
He leads me beside the still waters.
He restores my soul;
He leads me in the paths of righteousness
For His name's sake.

Yea, though I walk through the valley of the shadow of death,
I will fear no evil;
For You are with me;
Your rod and Your staff,
They comfort me.
You prepare a table before me
In the presence of my enemies;

You anoint my head with oil;
My cup runs over.
Surely goodness and mercy shall follow me
All the days of my life;
And I will dwell
In the house of the Lord forever.
Amen.

Praise Father, Son and Spirit.
For all that is light and lovely,
For the created, large and small,
For gifts of wisdom and wonder,
For all else in between.
Praise God who made us all.

Thank you, Lord God,
For Your presence and provision
In our journeys past and present.

At work, in home and community,
Grant us clearer vision to see You
Obedience as we walk with You
Patience to continue waiting on You
And a heart to receive more of You.

As we welcome Night's embrace
Lord be with us to guide us
Above us to raise us
Below us to uphold us
Before us to lead us
Behind us to shield us,
Illumine our hearts within
Renew our bodies without
Gather us in Your everlasting arms
This day and evermore.
This evening and evermore.***
Amen.

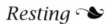

Resting

Tuesday

God Almighty

Morning – God Almighty 米

Hear, O Israel!
The Lord our God is one Lord:
And thou shalt love the Lord thy God with all thine heart,
And with all thy soul, and with all thy might.*

Silence

Lord God Almighty,
We acknowledge that You are in our midst.

We open our lives to Your love and guidance.
Bless our communities and loved ones.
Protect us with Your strength and peace.
We attend to Your presence and teaching today.

Psalm 19: 7-11 (NKJV)

The law of the Lord is perfect, converting the soul;
The testimony of the Lord is sure, making wise the simple;
The statutes of the Lord are right, rejoicing the heart;
The commandment of the Lord is pure, enlightening the eyes;

The fear of the Lord is clean, enduring forever;
The judgments of the Lord are true and righteous altogether.
More to be desired are they than gold...
Sweeter also than honey and the honeycomb.

Moreover by them Your servant is warned,
And in keeping them there is great reward.

Exodus 3: 1-8,10,13,14 (NKJV)

Now Moses was tending the flock...
and came to Horeb, the mountain of God.
And the Angel of the Lord appeared to him

in a flame of fire from the midst of a bush.
...And behold, the bush was not consumed.

...So when the Lord saw that he turned aside to look,
God called to him from the midst of the bush and said,

"Moses, Moses!" And he said, "Here I am."
..."Take your sandals off your feet,
for the place where you stand is holy ground."
... "I am the God of your father—the God of Abraham,
the God of Isaac, and the God of Jacob."

And Moses hid his face, for he was afraid to look upon God.

And the Lord said:
"I have surely seen the oppression of My people...
I know their sorrows.
So I have come down to deliver them
out of the hand of the Egyptians, and to bring them up
from that land to a good and large land,
to a land flowing with milk and honey...
Come now, therefore, and I will send you to Pharaoh
...to bring My people...out of Egypt."

..."Indeed, when I come to the children of Israel and say to them,
'The God of your fathers has sent me to you,' and they say to me,
'What is His name?' what shall I say to them?"

And God said to Moses, "I AM WHO I AM."

..."Thus you shall say to the children of Israel,
'I AM has sent me to you.'"

<u>Hymn: Praise to the Lord, the Almighty</u>

1. Praise to the Lord, the Almighty, the King of creation!
O my soul, praise Him, for He is thy health and salvation!
All ye who hear, now to His temple draw near;
Praise Him in glad adoration.

2. Praise to the Lord, Who over all things so wondrously reigneth,
Shelters thee under His wings, yea, so gently sustaineth!
Hast thou not seen how thy desires ever have been
Granted in what He ordaineth?

3. Praise to the Lord, O let all that is in me adore Him!
All that hath life and breath, come now with praises before Him.
Let the Amen sound from His people again,
Gladly for aye we adore Him.

Silence

Lord have mercy
Christ have mercy
Lord have mercy

Our Father who art in Heaven
Hallowed be Thy Name
Thy Kingdom come,
Thy will be done on earth
As it is in Heaven.

Give us this day our daily bread
And forgive us our trespasses
As we forgive those that trespass against us.
Lead us not into temptation
But deliver us from evil,
For Thine is the Kingdom
And the power and glory and honour,
Forever and ever.**
Amen.

Almighty God
Draw together Your elect
In one communion and fellowship
Through the sacrifice of Christ our Lord.

Give us grace to follow
Our 'fathers' and 'mothers' in the faith,
Who through the ages,
Model both virtue and life,

That we may receive the transformation, joy and gifts,
You have prepared for those who truly love You,
Through Lord Jesus Christ, Your Son,
In the unity of the Holy Spirit,
Holy Trinity, now and forever.

God give us grace to serve You all the days of our lives,
We and our households, choose to follow You Lord
In constancy, devotion and joy.

The Lord be with us this day and evermore.
Amen.

Afternoon – God Almighty ☀

Lord You have called us by Your Name
We are a people set apart and chosen,
The sheep of Your pastures.
Glory be Your Name.

Silence

Praise God from whom all blessings flow
Praise Him all creatures here below
Praise Him above ye heavenly hosts
Praise Father, Son and Holy Ghost.
Amen.

Psalm 91: 1-2, 4-6, 9-11 (NKJV)

He who dwells in the secret place of the Most High
Shall abide under the shadow of the Almighty.

I will say of the Lord, He is my refuge and my fortress;
My God, in Him I will trust.

He shall cover you with His feathers,
And under His wings you shall take refuge;
His truth shall be your shield and buckler.

You shall not be afraid of the terror by night,
Nor of the arrow that flies by day,
Nor of the pestilence that walks in darkness,
Nor of the destruction that lays waste at noonday.

Because you have made the Lord...your dwelling place,
No evil shall befall you...
For He shall give His angels charge over you,
To keep you in all your ways.

<u>Psalm 95: 6-7a (KJV)</u>

O come let us worship and bow down
Let us kneel before the Lord our God, our Maker.
For He is our God,
And we are the people of His pasture
And the sheep of His Hand.

Silence

Thank You Almighty God
In Your love we dwell today,
In Your strength we return to tasks at hand,
In Your peace we choose to rest.

The Lord be with us this day and evermore.
Amen.

Evening – God Almighty 米

Hear, O Israel!
The Lord our God is one Lord:
And thou shalt love the Lord thy God with all thine heart,
And with all thy soul, and with all thy might.*

Silence

Worship the Lord
In the power of His Name
In the beauty of His holiness.

In fellowship with all Your creation
We bow before You Lord Almighty.

1 Peter 1: 6-9; 2: 9-12 (NKJV)

In this you greatly rejoice, though now for a little while,
if need be, you have been grieved by various trials,
that the genuineness of your faith,
being much more precious than gold that perishes,
though it is tested by fire, may be found to praise,
honor, and glory at the revelation of Jesus Christ,
whom having not seen you love.
Though now you do not see Him, yet believing,
you rejoice with joy inexpressible and full of glory,
receiving the end of your faith—the salvation of your souls.

But you are a chosen generation,
a royal priesthood,
a holy nation,
His own special people,
that you may proclaim the praises of Him who called you
out of darkness
into His marvelous light;
who once were not a people
but are now the people of God,

who had not obtained mercy
but now have obtained mercy.

Beloved, I beg you as sojourners and pilgrims,
abstain from fleshly lusts which war against the soul,
having your conduct honorable among the Gentiles,
that when they speak against you as evildoers,
they may, by your good works which they observe,
glorify God in the day of visitation.

Hymn: Praise to the Lord, the Almighty

1. Praise to the Lord, Who doth prosper thy work and defend thee;
Surely His goodness and mercy here daily attend thee.
Ponder anew what the Almighty can do,
If with His love He befriend thee.

2. Praise to the Lord, Who, when tempests their warfare are
waging,
Who, when the elements madly around thee are raging,
Biddeth them cease, turneth their fury to peace,
Whirlwinds and waters assuaging.

3. Praise to the Lord, Who, when darkness of sin is abounding,
Who, when the godless do triumph, all virtue confounding,
Sheddeth His light, chaseth the horrors of night,
Saints with His mercy surrounding.

Silence

Our Father who art in Heaven
Hallowed be Thy Name
Thy Kingdom come,
Thy will be done on earth
As it is in Heaven.

Give us this day our daily bread
And forgive us our trespasses

As we forgive those that trespass against us.
Lead us not into temptation
But deliver us from evil,

For Thine is the Kingdom
And the power and glory and honour,
Forever and ever.
Amen.

Hearken people of God,
The Lord our God is one Lord:
Alleluia!

Thou shalt love the Lord thy God
With all thine heart,
With all thy soul,
And with all thy might.
Amen.

Now may the God of all grace,
Who calls us into covenant,
Unto His eternal glory
Through Christ Jesus,
Sustain us in suffering,
Strengthen us in character, and
Establish us in love.

The Lord be with us this night and evermore.
Amen.

 *Almighty*

Wednesday

Longing

Morning – Longing

As the hart pants for the running brooks
So my soul longs for You, my Lord.
Beloved Christ, come near.

Silence

Hear O loved of the Lord
Christ, our Beloved beckons.
Now draw near
Let His love fill you mind, body and spirit.

Lord Christ, we greet Thee this morn.
Sharpen our senses,
Guide us ever deeper into
Your transforming love.

<u>Psalm 42: 1-2, 8, 11 (NKJV)</u>

As the deer pants for the water brooks,
So pants my soul for You, O God.
My soul thirsts for God, for the living God...
Why are you cast down, O my soul?...

Hope in God, for I shall yet praise Him...
The Lord will command His lovingkindness in the daytime,
And in the night His song shall be with me—

A prayer to the God of my life.
Why are you cast down, O my soul?
And why are you disquieted within me?
Hope in God; for I shall yet praise Him...

<u>*Song of Songs 2: 1, 4, 10-13, 16 (NKJV)*</u>

I am the Rose of Sharon,
And the Lily of the valleys.

He brought me to the banqueting house,
And His banner over me *was* love.

My Beloved spoke,
"Rise up, My love, My fair one,
And come away.

For lo, the winter is past,
The rain is over and gone.
The flowers appear on the earth;
The time of singing has come,

And the voice of the turtledove is heard in our land.
The fig tree puts forth her green figs,
And the vines with the tender grape...

Rise up, My love, My fair one,
And come away!

My Beloved is mine, and I am His....

<u>*Hymn: Jesus, the Joy of Loving Hearts*</u>

1. Jesus the Joy of loving hearts
Our Fount of Life, the Light of men
From the best bliss that earth imparts
We turn unfilled to You again.

2. We taste You, oh our Living Bread
And long to feed upon You still
We drink from You, our Source, our Head
And thirst our souls from You to fill.

3. Our restless spirits yearn for You
Whatever lot or change may be
Glad when Your gracious smile we see
Bless'd when by faith we can cling to You.

Silence

Lord have mercy.
One thing have I desired of the Lord
That will I seek after;

Christ have mercy
That I may dwell in the house of the Lord
All the days of my life.

Lord have mercy
To behold the beauty of the Lord
To inquire in His temple.*
Thanks be to God.
Amen.

The Lord is my shepherd;
I shall not want.
He makes me to lie down in green pastures;
He leads me beside the still waters.
He restores my soul;
He leads me in the paths of righteousness
For His name's sake.

Yea, though I walk through the valley of the shadow of death,
I will fear no evil;
For You are with me;
Your rod and Your staff,
They comfort me.
You prepare a table before me
In the presence of my enemies;

You anoint my head with oil;
My cup runs over.
Surely goodness and mercy shall follow me
All the days of my life;
And I will dwell
In the house of the Lord forever.
Amen.

Praise You, O Lord
For it is Your love that seeks us
It is Your love that embraces us
It is Your love that suffers and bears
All our sin and frailty,
Your love redeems us
Your love invites us
Into Your love and life everlasting.

Just as the deer thirsts for running streams
So my soul longs for the Water of Life.
Beloved Christ, come near.

May you pursue the Lord more diligently,
Trusting that His love will cause you
To see with greater clarity,
Love with greater depth
Obey with greater ease.

The Lord be with us this day and evermore.
Amen.

Afternoon – Longing

Lord Jesus draw us today,
To dwell in Your presence and
Drink of Your sweet Water of Life.

Silence

Jesus the Joy of loving hearts.

We taste You, oh our Living Bread
And long to feed upon You still
We drink from You, our Source, our Head
And thirst our souls from You to fill.

Jesus the Joy of loving hearts.

Psalm 27: 4-6 (NKJV)

One thing I have desired of the Lord, that will I seek:

That I may dwell in the house of the Lord
All the days of my life,
To behold the beauty of the Lord,
And to inquire in His temple.

For in the time of trouble He shall hide me in His pavilion;
In the secret place of His tabernacle He shall hide me;
He shall set me high upon a rock.

And now my head shall be lifted up
above my enemies all around me;
Therefore I will offer sacrifices of joy in His tabernacle;

I will sing, yes, I will sing praises to the Lord.

Hymn: Jesus, the Joy of Loving Hearts

1. *Our restless spirits yearn for You*
Whatever lot or change may be
Glad when Your gracious smile we see
Bless'd when by faith we can cling to You.

Silence

Thank you Lord for Your invitation
To hunger and thirst after You.

Lord we ask now for strength
To cast our eyes and our hearts
Toward You.

Day by day,
May we learn and live
More rooted in Your love.
Amen.

Evening – Longing

Keep our hearts and souls
Still before You.
Prepare us Lord
For Your deeper work in us.

Silence

Lord Christ we wait on Thee.

To seal Your work this day,
As Love beckons to deeper waters.

Teach us this day to thirst.

Matthew 13: 44-46 (NIV)

The kingdom of heaven is like treasure hidden in a field.
When a man found it, he hid it again,
and then in his joy, went and sold all he had
and bought that field.

Again, the kingdom of heaven is like a merchant
looking for fine pearls.
When he found one of great value,
he went away and sold everything he had and bought it.

Luke 10: 38-42 (NIV)

As Jesus and his disciples were on their way...to a village
where a woman named Martha opened her home to him.
She had a sister called Mary,
who sat at the Lord's feet listening to what he said.

But Martha was distracted
by all the preparations that had to be made.

She came to him and asked,
"Lord, don't you care that my sister has left me
to do the work by myself?
Tell her to help me!"

"Martha, Martha," the Lord answered,
"You are worried and upset about many things,
but few things are needed—or indeed only one.

Mary has chosen what is better,
and it will not be taken away from her."

Hymn: Come, Thou Fount

1. Come, Thou Fount of every blessing,
Tune my heart to sing Thy grace;
Streams of mercy, never ceasing,
Call for songs of loudest praise.
Teach me some melodious sonnet,
Sung by flaming tongues above.
Praise the Fount! I'm fixed upon it,
Fount of Thy redeeming love.

2. O to grace how great a debtor
Daily I'm constrained to be!
Let Thy goodness, like a fetter,
Bind my wandering heart to Thee.
Prone to wander, Lord, I feel it,
Prone to leave the God I love;
Here's my heart, O take and seal it,
Seal it for Thy courts above.

Silence

The Lord is my shepherd;
I shall not want.
He makes me to lie down in green pastures;
He leads me beside the still waters.
He restores my soul;

He leads me in the paths of righteousness
For His name's sake.

Yea, though I walk through
the valley of the shadow of death,
I will fear no evil;
For You are with me;
Your rod and Your staff,
They comfort me.

You prepare a table before me
In the presence of my enemies;
You anoint my head with oil;
My cup runs over.

Surely goodness and mercy shall follow me
All the days of my life;
And I will dwell
In the house of the Lord forever.
Amen.

Lord have mercy.
One thing have I desired of the Lord
That will I seek after;

Christ have mercy
That I may dwell in the house of the Lord
All the days of my life.

Lord have mercy
To behold the beauty of the Lord
To inquire in His temple.

Thanks be to God.
Amen.

See beloved of the Lord
Christ, our Beloved beckons
Now draw near

Feel, sense, and embrace
His love for you.

As the hart pants for the running brooks
so my soul longs for You, my Lord.
Beloved Christ, come near.

As we welcome Night's embrace
Lord Christ be with us to guide us
Above us to raise us
Below us to uphold us
Before us to lead us
Behind us to shield us,
Illumine our hearts within
Renew our bodies without
Gather us in Your everlasting arms
This day and evermore.
This evening and evermore.
Amen.

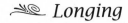 *Longing*

Thursday

Jesus Christ

Morning – Jesus Christ 🕊

Emmanuel, God with us.
Lord Jesus, waken us this morn
Beloved Friend, speak and live
Through us this day.

Silence

Christ, our Light,
Illumine and guide us.
Christ, our Shield,
Overshadow and shelter us.
Christ be under us,
Christ be over us,
Christ be beside us,
On the left and on the right,
*Christ be within and without us.**

<u>Psalm 121 (NKJV)</u>

I will lift up my eyes to the hills
From whence comes my help?
My help comes from the Lord,
Who made heaven and earth.

He will not allow your foot to be moved;
He who keeps you will not slumber.
Behold, He who keeps Israel
Shall neither slumber nor sleep.

The Lord is your keeper;
The Lord is your shade at your right hand.
The sun shall not strike you by day,
Nor the moon by night.

The Lord shall preserve you from all evil;
He shall preserve your soul.

The Lord shall preserve your going out and your coming in
From this time forth, and even forevermore.

Isaiah 9: 2, 6, 7 (NKJV)

The people who walked in darkness have seen a great light;
Those who dwelt in the land of the shadow of death,
Upon them a light has shined.

For unto us a Child is born, unto us a Son is given;
And the government will be upon His shoulder.
And His name will be called Wonderful, Counselor,
Mighty God, Everlasting Father, Prince of Peace.

Of the increase of His government and peace there will be no end,
Upon the throne of David and over His kingdom,
To order it and establish it with judgment and justice
From that time forward, even forever.

The zeal of the Lord of hosts will perform this.

Hymn: Be Thou My Vision

1. Be Thou my Vision, O Lord of my heart
Naught be all else to me save that Thou art
Thou my best thought by day or by night
Waking or sleeping Thy presence my light.

2. Be Thou my breastplate, my sword for the fight
Be Thou my whole armour, be Thou my true might
Be Thou my soul's shelter, be Thou my strong tower
O, raise Thou me heav'nward, great Power of my power.

3. Riches I heed not nor man's empty praise
Thou mine inheritance now and always
Thou and Thou only first in my heart
High King of heaven my Treasure Thou art.

Silence

Christ who died for our sins, forgive the penitent.
(Pause for inward confession of personal sin, and to forgive those who have sinned against us.)
Lord have mercy.

Christ who bore our grief, comfort the sorrowing.
(Pause to intercede for ourselves or individuals who are grieving.)
Lord have mercy.

Lord who thirsted, relieve the parched and hungry.
(Pause to pray silently for the physically, emotionally, and spiritually hungry in our lives and communities.)
Lord have mercy.

Christ forsaken, comfort the sad and lonely.
(Pause to pray for ourselves and/or others who feel isolated and alone.)
Lord have mercy.

Lord scorned and rejected, uphold the outcast and dispossessed.
(Pause to intercede for ourselves and/or individuals who may be abandoned, rejected or alienated.)
Lord have mercy.

Christ who suffered, be Strength to the weak.
(Pause to silently pray for ourselves and/or others who are weak or broken.)
Lord have mercy.

Lord crucified and risen, raise us to glory.
Christ have mercy.

Our Father who art in Heaven
Hallowed be Thy Name
Thy Kingdom come,
Thy will be done on earth
As it is in Heaven.

Give us this day our daily bread
And forgive us our trespasses
As we forgive those that trespass against us.
Lead us not into temptation
But deliver us from evil,
For Thine is the Kingdom
And the power and glory and honour,
Forever and ever.
Amen

Brother Christ, walk with us,
As You once did, on the road to Emmaus.
Lord Christ, teach us Your ways.
Gentle Savior, help us forgive as You forgive,
Shepherd King, guard our paths,
Lead us in Your grace.

Brother Christ, Counselor Friend,
Guide us this day.
Shepherd King, Healer Kind,
Open our hearts to Your love.
Prince of Peace, Gentle Savior,
Grant us a glimpse of eternity.

The grace of our Lord Jesus Christ, the love of God,
And the fellowship of the Holy Spirit
Be with us all forevermore.
Amen.

Afternoon – Jesus Christ 🕊

Emmanuel, God with us,
In the expected tasks of life
And unexpected movements,
Anchor us today in Your presence.

Silence

Praise God from whom all blessings flow
Praise Him all creatures here below
Praise Him above ye heavenly hosts
Praise Father, Son and Holy Ghost.
Amen.

Luke 1: 76-79 (NKJV)

And you, child, will be called the prophet of the Highest;
For you will go before the face of the Lord
to prepare His ways,
To give knowledge of salvation to His people
By the remission of their sins,

Through the tender mercy of our God,
With which the Dayspring from on high has visited us;
To give light to those who sit in darkness
and the shadow of death,
To guide our feet into the way of peace.

Hymn: O Come, O Come, Emmanuel

1. O come, O come, Emmanuel,
And ransom captive Israel,
That mourns in lonely exile here
Until the Son of God appear.

Refrain
Rejoice! Rejoice! Emmanuel
Shall come to thee, O Israel.

2. O come, Thou Day-spring, come and cheer
Our spirits by Thine advent here;
Disperse the gloomy clouds of night,
And death's dark shadows put to flight.
Refrain

Silence

O come, Desire of Nations, bind
In one the hearts of all mankind;
Bid Thou our sad divisions cease,
And be Thyself our King of Peace.

The Lord be with us this day and evermore.
Amen.

Evening – Jesus Christ ❧

Behold, the Lamb of God
Who takes away the sin of the world.

Silence

Alleluia, Christ came to us.
Rejoice O silent planet,
Sing with the heavenly hosts
He lived, in favor with God and man,
He suffered, died and rose again.

Alleluia, Christ is coming again.
Rejoice O silent planet,
Your redemption and recreation is at hand.
Soon your celebration will resound.

Matthew 3: 13, 15-17 (NKJV)

Then Jesus came from Galilee to John
at the Jordan to be baptized...

When He had been baptized,
Jesus came up immediately from the water;
and behold, the heavens were opened to Him,
and He saw the Spirit of God descending like a dove
and alighting upon Him.

And suddenly a voice came from heaven, saying,
"This is My beloved Son, in whom I am well pleased."

Luke 4: 1, 14, 16-21 (NIV)

Jesus, full of the Holy Spirit, left the Jordan
and was led by the Spirit into the wilderness,
where for forty days He was tempted by the devil.

Jesus returned to Galilee in the power of the Spirit,
and news about Him spread through the whole countryside.
He went to Nazareth...on the Sabbath day
He went into the synagogue, as was His custom.
He stood up to read...

"The Spirit of the Lord is on me,
because He has anointed Me
to proclaim good news to the poor.

He has sent Me to proclaim freedom for the prisoners
and recovery of sight for the blind,
to set the oppressed free,
to proclaim the year of the Lord's favor."

...The eyes of everyone in the synagogue were fastened on Him.

..."Today this scripture is fulfilled in your hearing."

Hymn: Be Thou My Vision

1. Be Thou my Wisdom, and Thou my true Word.
I ever with Thee and Thou with me, Lord.
Thou my great Father, I Thy true son.
Thou in me dwelling and I with Thee one.

2. Be Thou my Vision, O Lord of my heart.
Naught be all else to me, save that Thou art.
Thou my best thought, by day or by night.
Waking or sleeping Thy presence my light.

Silence

Christ who died for our sins, forgive the penitent.
(Pause for intercessory prayer.)
Lord have mercy.

Christ who bore our grief, comfort the sorrowing.
(Pause for intercessory prayer.)
Lord have mercy.

Lord who thirsted, relieve the parched and hungry.
(Pause for intercessory prayer.)
Lord have mercy.

Christ forsaken, comfort the sad and lonely.
(Pause for intercessory prayer.)
Lord have mercy.

Lord scorned and rejected, uphold the outcast and dispossessed.
(Pause for intercessory prayer.)
Lord have mercy.

Christ who suffered, be Strength to the weak.
(Pause for intercessory prayer.)
Lord have mercy.

Lord crucified and risen, raise us to glory.
Christ have mercy.

Our Father who art in Heaven
Hallowed be Thy Name
Thy Kingdom come,
Thy will be done on earth
As it is in Heaven.

Give us this day our daily bread
And forgive us our trespasses
As we forgive those that trespass against us.
Lead us not into temptation
But deliver us from evil,
For Thine is the Kingdom
And the power and glory and honour,
Forever and ever.
Amen.

In the darkening of dusk,
Embrace His gift!

*O what manner of love
He has bestowed upon us.*

Rejoice again with loving gratitude,
That we bear the mark of the cross
And the seal of His glorious name.

As we welcome Night's embrace
Lord Christ be with us to guide us
Above us to raise us
Below us to uphold us
Before us to lead us
Behind us to shield us,
Illumine our hearts within
Renew our bodies without
Gather us in Your everlasting arms
This day and evermore.
This evening and evermore.
Amen.

Christ

Friday

Abiding

Morning – Abiding ☙☙

Lord God, open our hearts.
Lord Christ, we welcome Your presence,
Lord Spirit, we receive Your transforming work,
One movement at a time.

Silence

We abide in Thee, O Lord,
For Thou art Life, Joy and Peace.

Grant us faith and courage
As lambs under Thy watchful eyes,
To follow where we cannot yet see.

As a patient lies quiet to a surgeon's knife,
To trust Your healing touch.
In ways we may not yet understand,

We abide ever in Thy life and grace, O Lord.

Psalm 145: 13b-21 (NIV)

The Lord is trustworthy in all He promises and faithful in all He does.
The Lord upholds all who fall and lifts up all who are bowed down.
The eyes of all look to You and
You give them their food at the proper time.
You open Your hand and satisfy the desires of every living thing.

The Lord is righteous in all His ways and faithful in all He does.
The Lord is near to all who call on Him,
to all who call on Him in truth.
He fulfills the desires of those who fear Him;
He hears their cry and saves them.
The Lord watches over all who love Him,
but all the wicked He will destroy...
Let every creature praise His holy name forever and ever.

2 Chronicles 6: 1-2, 14, 16, 18-21, 38-39, 41 (NKJV)

Then Solomon spoke:
"The Lord said He would dwell in the dark cloud.

I have surely built You an exalted house,
And a place for You to dwell in forever."

... "Lord God of Israel, there is no God in heaven
or on earth like You, who keep Your covenant and mercy
with Your servants who walk before You with all their hearts...
Therefore, Lord God of Israel, now keep what You promised
Your servant David my father...

"...Behold, heaven and the heaven of heavens cannot contain You.
How much less this temple which I have built!
Yet regard the prayer of Your servant...
...that Your eyes may be open toward this temple day and night...
that You may hear the prayer
which Your servant makes toward this place.
And may You hear the supplications of Your servant
and of Your people Israel, when they pray toward this place.

...and when they return to You with all their heart
and with all their soul in the land of their captivity...
then hear... and forgive Your people.

"Now therefore arise, O Lord God, to Your resting place...
Let Your priests, O Lord God, be clothed with salvation,
And let Your saints rejoice in goodness.

Hymn: May the Mind of Christ, My Savior

1. May the mind of Christ, my Savior,
Live in me from day to day,
By His love and power controlling
All I do and say.

2. May the peace of God my Father
Rule my life in everything,
That I may be calm to comfort
Sick and sorrowing.

Silence

Lord hear us, we pray
For your sheep, those lost, found, and wounded.
(Pause to offer silent prayers for our churches and neighborhoods.)
Lord have mercy.

For your shepherds, faithful, frail and worn.
(Pause to offer silent prayers for our spiritual leaders, parents and mentors.)
Lord have mercy.

For those who serve in conflict and adversity
(Pause to pray for believers and leaders serving in areas of conflict and persecution.)
Lord have mercy.

For the poor, the broken, the betrayed, and the powerless.
(Pause to offer silent prayers for such individuals and groups around the world.)
Lord hear us, we pray.

Thank you Lord for hearing us.

The Lord is my shepherd; I shall not want.

He maketh me to lie down in green pastures:
He leadeth me beside the still waters.
He restoreth my soul:
He leadeth me in the paths of righteousness for His name's sake.

Yea, though I walk through the valley of the shadow of death,
I will fear no evil: for Thou art with me;
Thy rod and Thy staff they comfort me.

Thou preparest a table before me in the presence of mine enemies:
Thou anointest my head with oil; my cup runneth over.
Surely goodness and mercy shall follow me all the days of my life:
and I will dwell in the house of the Lord for ever.
Amen.

Lord be with us.

In our work, toil and travail
Lord sustain us.
In our pain, weakness and sorrowing
Lord embrace us.
In our transgressions and confession
Lord forgive us.
In our darkness and brokenness
Lord heal us.

Lord be with us.

May the love of the Great Shepherd
Bind your heart, mind and soul to Him.
May His peace and power
Surround and ground you this day.

Glory be to the Father
And to the Son
And to the Holy Ghost
As it was in the beginning is now
*And shall be forever more.**
Amen.

Afternoon – Abiding ᕙᕗ

As the sun marks the day,
Our hearts incline to Thine,
Our ears hearken to Thine voice and
Our hands raise to Thee in praise.

Silence

Praise God from whom all blessings flow
Praise Him all creatures here below
Praise Him above ye heavenly hosts
Praise Father, Son and Holy Ghost.
Amen.

<u>Luke 13: 10-13 (New Living Translation)</u>

One Sabbath day as Jesus was teaching in a synagogue,
He saw a woman who had been crippled by an evil spirit.
She had been bent double for eighteen years
and was unable to stand up straight.

When Jesus saw her, He called her over and said,
"Dear woman, you are healed of your sickness!"
Then He touched her, and instantly she could stand straight.
How she praised God!

<u>Hymn: May the Mind of Christ, My Savior</u>

1. May the Word of God dwell richly
In my heart from hour to hour,
So that all may see I triumph
Only through His power.

2. May I run the race before me,
Strong and brave to face the foe,
Looking only unto Jesus
As I onward go.

Silence

Glory be to the Father
And to the Son
And to the Holy Ghost
As it was in the beginning is now
And shall be forever more.
Amen.

Evening – Abiding 🦅🦅

As we greet Thee this hour,
We are distracted with life;
Prone to wander and lose sight of Thee.
Weighed down in heart and body, pressed in mind,
Come restore, heal and transform us today.

Silence

Loving God, be Thou our Anchor
We cling to Thee.
Be Thou our Dwelling
We shelter in Thee.
Be Thou our Spring of Life
We drink of Thee.
Be Thou our Eternal Vine.

John 15: 1, 4-11 (NASB)

"I am the true vine, and My Father is the vinedresser.
Abide in Me, and I in you...

I am the vine, you are the branches;
he who abides in Me and I in him,
he bears much fruit,
for apart from Me you can do nothing....

If you abide in Me, and My words abide in you,
ask whatever you wish,
and it will be done for you.

My Father is glorified by this, that you bear much fruit,
and so prove to be My disciples.

Just as the Father has loved Me,
I have also loved you;

Abide in My love.
If you keep My commandments, you will abide in My love;

...These things I have spoken to you
so that My joy may be in you,
and that your joy may be made full.

<u>Hymn: May the Mind of Christ, My Savior</u>

1. May the love of Jesus fill me
As the waters fill the sea;
Him exalting, self abasing,
This is victory.

2. May His beauty rest upon me,
As I seek the lost to win,
And may they forget the channel,
Seeing only Him.

Silence

The Lord is my shepherd; I shall not want.

He maketh me to lie down in green pastures:
He leadeth me beside the still waters.
He restoreth my soul:

He leadeth me in the paths of righteousness for His name's sake.
Yea, though I walk through the valley of the shadow of death,
I will fear no evil: for Thou art with me;
Thy rod and Thy staff they comfort me.

Thou preparest a table before me in the presence of mine enemies:
Thou anointest my head with oil; my cup runneth over.

Surely goodness and mercy shall follow me all the days of my life:
and I will dwell in the house of the Lord for ever.
Amen.

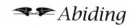

Where we have been unloving in choice, deed and thought.
(Pause to offer silent confessions for our frailties and failings.)
Lord, in your mercy, forgive us.

Where we bear unseen brokenness and sickness in body, mind and soul.
(Pause to pray for greater self-awareness and health for ourselves and others.)
Lord, in your lovingkindness, heal us.

In gaps of needs unmet and hunger unsatisfied.
(Pause to pray for provision of personal and communal needs.)
Lord, in your goodness, fill us.

May the love of the Great Shepherd
Bind your heart, mind and soul to Him.
May His peace and power
Surround and ground you this day.

Glory be to the Father
And to the Son
And to the Holy Ghost
As it was in the beginning is now
And shall be forever more.
Amen.

Abiding

Saturday

Holy Spirit

Morning – Holy Spirit ᵔ—

Enter in, Spirit of God.
Come now, dance in our lives,
Awake, quicken, revive
Purify us we pray.

Silence

Renew us, soul to cell.
Comforter, Counselor, Healer
Come now, come near.
Transform us within and without.
Open our eyes to see Your truth,
Stir our hearts to worship You,
Draw us with Your tune.
Purify us we pray.

Psalm 139: 1-3, 5-12, 14a (NKJV)

O Lord, You have searched me and known me.
You know my sitting down and my rising up;
You understand my thought afar off.
You comprehend my path...are acquainted with all my ways.

You have hedged me behind and before,
And laid Your hand upon me.
Such knowledge is too wonderful for me;
It is high, I cannot attain it.

Where can I go from Your Spirit?
Or where can I flee from Your presence?
If I ascend into heaven, You are there;
If I make my bed in hell, behold, You are there.

If I take the wings of the morning,
And dwell in the uttermost parts of the sea,
Even there Your hand shall lead me,
And Your right hand shall hold me.

If I say, "Surely the darkness shall fall on me,"
Even the night shall be light about me;
Indeed, the darkness shall not hide from You...
The darkness and the light are both alike to You.

I will praise You, for I am fearfully and wonderfully made.

1 Samuel 1: 10, 11, 20, 24, 26-28 (NASB)

She, greatly distressed, prayed to the Lord...made a vow and said,
"O Lord of hosts, if You will...remember me,
and...give Your maidservant a son,
then I will give him to the Lord all the days of his life,
and a razor shall never come on his head."

It came about in due time, after Hannah had conceived,
that she gave birth to a son;
and she named him Samuel, saying,
"Because I have asked him of the Lord."

Now when she had weaned him, she took him up with her,
with a three-year-old bull and one ephah of flour and a jug of wine,
and brought him to the house of the Lord in Shiloh,
although the child was young.

She said, "Oh, my lord...I am the woman who stood here
...praying to the Lord.
For this boy I prayed, and the Lord has given me my petition...
So I have also dedicated him to the Lord;
as long as he lives he is dedicated to the Lord."
And he worshipped the Lord there.

Hymn: Spirit Divine

1. Spirit divine, attend our prayer,
And make our heart Thy home;
Descend with all Thy gracious power;
Come, Holy Spirit, come.

2. Come as the light, to us reveal,
The truth we long to know;
Reveal the narrow path of right,
The way of duty show.

3. Come as the dove, and spread Thy wings,
The wings of peaceful love;
And let Thy Church on earth become
Blest as Thy Church above.

Silence

My heart exults in the Lord,
For He has saved me from my enemies.

Holy Lord, our rock and salvation.
And there is none on earth like You.
Our lives rest in Your hand.

You raise the low and humble the proud.
You strengthen the weak, and break the mighty.
You feed the hungry and heal the barren.
You lift up the poor among the princes.

You protect the godly and silence the wicked.
You strengthen the ruler and exalt Your anointed ones.
Earth to heaven, heaven to earth, Your throne endures forever.
In Your hands are power, knowledge, judgment and glory.

My heart exults in the Lord,
For He has saved me from my enemies.*
Amen.

Lord have mercy.
Spirit have mercy.
Lord have mercy.

Holy Spirit, grant us grace,
To see Your hand at work in us.

Forgive our sins.
In Your mercy, help us forgive.

Strengthen our frailties and anchor our hearts.
Grant us a gentle spirit towards other's flaws.

Regenerate us in body, mind and spirit.
Train us to be a fount of Your blessing.

My help cometh from the Lord who made heaven and earth.
The Lord is Thy keeper;
The Lord is Thy shade at thy right hand.
The sun shall not strike thee by day,
Nor the moon by night.
Behold, He who watches over Thee
Neither slumbers nor sleeps.**

Afternoon – Holy Spirit ❧

Spirit of God, we exult Thee.
Spirit of Life, we adore Thee.
Fire of God, we welcome Thee.
Alleluia.

Silence

Praise God from whom all blessings flow
Praise Him all creatures here below
Praise Him above ye heavenly hosts
Praise Father, Son and Holy Ghost.
Amen.

<u>*1 Samuel 16: 7, 11-13 (NASB)*</u>

But the Lord said to Samuel,
"Do not look at his appearance or at the height of his stature,
because I have rejected him;
for God sees not as man sees,
for man looks at the outward appearance,
but the Lord looks at the heart."

And Samuel said to Jesse,
"Are these all the children?"

And he said, "There remains yet the youngest,
and behold, he is tending the sheep."...
So he sent and brought him in.

Now he was ruddy, with beautiful eyes
and a handsome appearance.

And the Lord said,
"Arise, anoint him; for this is he."

Then Samuel...anointed him in the midst of his brothers;
and the Spirit of the Lord came mightily upon David
from that day forward.

<u>Hymn: Spirit Divine</u>

1. Come as the fire and purge our hearts
Like sacrificial flame,
Till our whole soul an offering be
In love's redeeming name.

2. Come as the dove, and spread Thy wings,
The wings of peaceful love;
And let Thy Church on earth become
Blest as Thy Church above.

Silence

My heart exults in the Lord,
For He has saved me from my enemies.

Holy Lord, our rock and salvation
And there is none on earth like You.

Our lives lie in Your hand.
You raise the low and humble the proud.

You strengthen the weak, and break the mighty
You feed the hungry and heal the barren.

You lift up the poor among the princes.
You protect the godly and silence the wicked.

You strengthen the ruler and exalt Your anointed ones.
Earth to heaven, heaven to earth, Your throne endures forever.

In Your hands are power, knowledge, judgment and glory.

My heart exults in the Lord,
*For He has saved me from my enemies.**
Amen.

My help cometh from the Lord
who made heaven and earth.

The Lord is Thy keeper;
The Lord is Thy shade at thy right hand.
The sun shall not strike thee by day,
Nor the moon by night.
Behold, He who watches over Thee
Neither slumbers nor sleeps.**

Evening – Holy Spirit

Spirit of God, from the beginning of time,
God uncreated, from the foundations of the universe,
In Thee we live and move and have our being.

Silence

Spirit God, revive our lives and communities
Spirit sent, restore Your creation.
Holy Ghost, baptize and seal us for Your Kingdom.

Acts 1: 4-8; 2: 1-6, 12 (NKJV)

And being assembled together with them,
He commanded them not to depart from Jerusalem,
but to wait for the promise of the Father...
...But you shall receive power
when the Holy Spirit has come upon you;
and you shall be witnesses to Me in Jerusalem,
and in all Judea and Samaria, and to the end of the earth.

When the day of Pentecost had fully come,
they were all with one accord in one place.
And suddenly there came a sound from heaven,
as of a rushing mighty wind,
and it filled the whole house where they were sitting.

Then there appeared to them divided tongues, as of fire,
and one sat upon each of them.
And they were all filled with the Holy Spirit and began to speak
with other tongues, as the Spirit gave them utterance.

And there were dwelling in Jerusalem Jews,
devout men, from every nation under heaven.
And when this sound occurred, the multitude...were confused,
because everyone heard them speak in his own language.
So they were all amazed and perplexed....

Hymn: Spirit Divine

1. Come as the wind, O Breath of God!
O Pentecostal grace!
Come, make Thy great salvation known,
Wide as the human race.

2. Spirit divine, attend our prayer;
Make a lost world Thy home;
Descend with all Thy gracious powers,
O come, great Spirit, come.

Silence

My heart exults in the Lord,
For He has saved me from my enemies.

Holy Lord, our rock and salvation
And there is none on earth like You.

Our lives lie in Your hand.
You raise the low and humble the proud.

You strengthen the weak, and break the mighty.
You feed the hungry and heal the barren.
You lift up the poor among the princes.

You protect the godly and silence the wicked.
You strengthen the ruler and exalt Your anointed ones.
Earth to heaven, heaven to earth, Your throne endures forever.
In Your hands are power, knowledge, judgment and glory.

My heart exults in the Lord,
For He has saved me from my enemies.**
Amen.

Lord have mercy.
Spirit have mercy.
Lord have mercy.

Holy Spirit, grant us grace
To see Your hand at work in us.
Forgive our sins.
In Your mercy, help us forgive.

Strengthen our frailties and anchor our hearts.
Grant us a gentle spirit towards other's flaws.
Regenerate us in body, mind and spirit.
Train us to be a fount of Your blessing.

The Lord shall preserve you from all evil;
He shall preserve your soul.
The Lord shall preserve your going out and your coming in
From this time forth, and even forevermore.**
Amen.

Spirit ⌀—

4

Ways to Use this Guide

This prayer guide is designed to be accessible to those who are becoming familiar with daily offices, and versatile in application. The daily prayer devotions may be used in individual and group contexts. Suggestions for both types of settings are offered here.

Individual Prayer Rhythm

In light of an already full and busy life, we desire the benefit of a prayer rhythm to help us focus on Christ, to order our day beyond sporadic or short prayer times. Pausing throughout our day and week with this prayer guide can facilitate such a desired awareness, and strengthen our prayer life.

Whether we are struggling with a hectic schedule in general, or our private prayer specifically, we can grow our capacity for personal prayer beyond offering a list of prayer requests. We recommend using this guide for three months. Observe what happens in the process. Begin with at least one office a day, three times a week.

Individual Retreats

Perhaps our desire leans towards spending a focused time with God. A retreat may be a useful setting to seek guidance, rest, or just an extended time of sitting at Jesus' feet. Retreats may be taken for a variety of circumstances, ranging from a regular practice to enhance our spiritual life, to finding rest in difficult transitions, or recovery from a crisis. Retreats are often encouraged for emotional and spiritual health, as well as for discernment.

Whatever the focus or theme of a retreat, we recommend this guide as a supplement in your retreat. Whether a retreat is a day or a month in length, this prayer guide may be adapted for a planned retreat setting. Observing a daily office may provide a helpful framework. On retreat, portions of this guide may be integrated into a daily routine.

Group Settings

Observing a daily office as a group of believers binds hearts, minds and spirits in community. In the setting of a bible study or a home fellowship group, allow this daily office to serve as a way to deepen community connections, and grow your corporate worship practices.

In a similar vein, this guide may be a means of fresh engagement in corporate worship in a larger group such as a new church plant, a college chapel or a conference setting.

Consider the possible wonder and efficacy of the daily office, the creative tapestry of spiritual practices that it offers as we engage it daily, and above all, the encounter it offers of God with us.

Just as our rhythms of Sabbath and Sunday worship incorporate many threads, praying the daily offices provide day-to-day moments of sacred silence, rest, Scripture meditation, prayer, worship, community witness, and celebration.

5

Hints for Anchoring a Rhythm

Initial Thoughts as You Begin

1. Do some simple planning before diving into the practice. It can be as simple as a few minutes of sketching out a plan.

2. Plan at least two months of regular and consistent use.

3. Identify the three key main motivators for using this prayer guide.

4. Identify a quiet place or uninterrupted space to whisper or speak your offices.

5. Identify the three main obstacles you are likely to encounter.

6. Consider two options to overcome each obstacle.

7. Share your plan with one or two trusted individuals, such as spiritual friends or mentors.

8. Plan to celebrate your results, perhaps at the end of three weeks of praying the offices, with a loved one (e.g., your favorite treat).

9. If you already have a full plate, consider re-purposing an existing spiritual task or time.

10. Life happens so build in some margins.

11. Plan for the unexpected glitch (e.g., work in an extra office at a time other than the planned schedule, in case you have to miss an office).

12. In the case of regular misses during the two months, evaluate and change your plan to something more manageable.

13. Avoid negative self-talk and criticism.

14. Ask the Lord to provide whatever you need to complete this task.

15. Relax and enjoy it.

Community Considerations

Consider what prayer pattern is sustainable for you before beginning. The involvement of family and friends at some level can make the difference in our prayer life. It will also impact them as we model a priority for prayer to those close to us.

Life and yearly seasons may impact our rhythm and success in using the daily offices. People's schedules may change with work projects and seasons, some busier and more tiring than others. Be realistic in planning.

Family considerations, like having young children, or having different winter or summer life routines, can impact a desired rhythm. We may invite a family member or someone in our spiritual community to participate or join us. Solicit their prayer and support.

Dispositional Considerations

Let natural rhythms or dispositions inform our prayer practice.
Nature lovers may find it easier to pray in the garden or a park. Others may prefer a closet. More introverted individuals may engage in longer silences without much effort. Extroverts may prefer shorter silent pauses.

Reflect on the part of the week and day that may work better in our schedules. Reflect on the frequency we want to keep and how much time it will take. If one is not a morning person, begin with just an evening office. If three offices a day seems too much, start with a morning and evening office. If offices everyday seem overwhelming, consider doing them only on weekdays and rest for the weekends.

Our recommendation is to begin with at least one office a day, three days a week. Start as soon as possible lest procrastination saps what resolve we have. However, in the case of a big transition or busy season, plan to begin later when routines are more stable and margins can be found.

Everyone is different, so allow the Spirit to guide us on our planning. In matters of the soul and heart, we recommend being gentle with ourselves.

Rules of Thumb for Forming Habits

Habits are dynamic not static. What is daily or regular has transforming power.

Repetition and simplicity are powerful principles because they are part of the natural law God has built into creation, including human beings. They give the Holy Spirit and our spirits room to breathe and move. Contrary to popular belief, more is not always better, and constant change may derail or stifle a budding habit.

This guide is intentionally short and simple, only a week in length. The seven-day pattern, repeated over weeks and months, allows a rhythm to emerge with less force and more freedom from the heart.

The repetition of simple texts and short prayers helps God's Word and spiritual wisdom to seep in more deeply. In time they will shape our inward disposition and spiritual character.

Persistence makes permanent. Whatever change you make, be sure to give it a few months for the change to anchor and bear fruit. Realize that any change requires about two to three months of regular observance to become internalized. So allow margin for exploration and expectation.

Space matters. A physical space is just as important as a mental and emotional space. Consider preparing a prayer space, such as a desk or armchair that is conducive for prayer. Outside the home, find or create a space that is quiet, uncluttered and free from distractions. The use of simple objects or symbols, such as a cross, flame, flower or Bible, can adequately transform a space. Any of these objects can also help us focus in light of stress or distraction.

Margins for Life Considerations

Seasons of sorrow and pain may surprise and weigh on us, when praying seem more urgent and yet more challenging. In times of difficulty, pain or grief, our physical, emotional and spiritual resources may be stretched.

Whenever we navigate a loss or crisis, prayer becomes even more essential. In such seasons of suffering or recovery, this prayer guide may serve as a light through the darkness that besets us, a means to overcome inner lethargy or resistance we encounter.

When God seems silent or hidden, maintaining our prayer life may be an agonizing struggle. In these seasons our prayers may be encouraged with a structural support such as a prayer guide. So prayer rhythms may also be unforced rhythms of grace, which may be just what we need to anchor us in harsh seasons.

Many have found it difficult to pray in their darker times and have felt guilty. Because living out a prayer rhythm is soul work, it requires inner resources to sustain it. In such challenging seasons, allow permission to do what you can. Avoid undue pressure and force at these times if your find yourself unable to keep a stable prayer practice.

Ministry Considerations

For some of us, leaders or ministers who are less familiar with praying the offices, it may be best to first establish this practice personally, before any use of it in our ministry or as program for a larger group. We recommend maintaining this practice privately for a year or two, perhaps longer, as the Lord leads.

As many through the ages can attest to this, there is encouragement and power in praying the offices in community. We encourage leaders and ministers to find others, a group of like-minded individuals with a similar longing to grow their prayer life, who also wish to pray the offices within the support of the group.

For many in full-time or voluntary ministry, ministry considerations can hamper our best intentions. For ministers and pastors, personal prayer time, besides intercession, sermon preparation or prayer ministry to others, may be an important need that is overlooked. Depending on the individual, this may be a need to be prioritized and negotiated in the midst of many ministry demands.

In the midst of louder voices and demands, let us cling tenaciously to this truth, that a deepening communion with God is a non-negotiable for all believers, especially those who serve as shepherds of God's flock.

6

Other Helps

Additional Prayers

Doxology (spoken or sung)

Praise God from whom all blessings flow
Praise Him all creatures here below
Praise Him above ye heavenly hosts
Praise Father, Son and Holy Ghost. Amen.

Gloria Patri

Glory be to the Father
And to the Son
And to the Holy Ghost
As it was in the beginning is now
And shall be forever more. Amen.

Psalm 23 (KJV)

The Lord is my shepherd;
I shall not want.
He maketh me to lie down in green pastures:
He leadeth me beside the still waters.
He restoreth my soul:
He leadeth me in the paths of righteousness for his name's sake.
Yea, though I walk through the valley of the shadow of death,
I will fear no evil:
For Thou art with me; Thy rod and Thy staff they comfort me.
Thou preparest a table before me in the presence of mine enemies:

Thou anointest my head with oil; my cup runneth over.
Surely goodness and mercy shall follow me all the days of my life:
And I will dwell in the house of the Lord forever.

Psalm 121 (NKJV)

I will lift up my eyes to the hills
From whence comes my help?
My help comes from the Lord,
Who made heaven and earth.
He will not allow your foot to be moved;
He who keeps you will not slumber.
Behold, He who keeps Israel shall neither slumber nor sleep.
The Lord is your keeper;
The Lord is your shade at your right hand.
The sun shall not strike you by day, nor the moon by night.
The Lord shall preserve you from all evil;
He shall preserve your soul.
The Lord shall preserve your going out and your coming in
From this time forth, and even forevermore.

Numbers 6: 24-26 (Adapted)

The Lord bless you, and keep you:
The Lord make His face shine upon you,
And be gracious unto you:
The Lord lift up His countenance upon you,
And give you peace.

2 Corinthians 13:14 (Adapted)

The grace of the Lord Jesus Christ,
And the love of God,
And the communion of the Holy Spirit
Be with you all. Amen.

<u>2 Corinthians 13:14 (Option)</u>

The grace of our Lord Jesus Christ,
The love of God,
And the fellowship of the Holy Spirit
Be with us all forever more.
The blessing of the Father
And of the Son
And of the Holy Spirit
Be with us and remain with us
Now and always.
Amen.

Creeds

Apostles' Creed

I believe in God, the Father Almighty, creator of heaven and earth;

I believe in Jesus Christ, His only Son, our Lord.
He was conceived by the power of the Holy Spirit
and born of the virgin Mary.
He suffered under Pontius Pilate,
was crucified, died, and was buried.
He descended to the dead.
On the third day He rose again.
He ascended into heaven,
and is seated at the right hand of the Father.
He will come again to judge the living and the dead.

I believe in the Holy Spirit,
the holy catholic[1] (Christian) Church,
the communion of saints,
the forgiveness of sins
the resurrection of the body,
and the life everlasting. Amen.

Nicene Creed

We believe in one God, the Father, the Almighty,
Maker of heaven and earth, of all that is, seen and unseen.

We believe in one Lord, Jesus Christ, the only Son of God,
eternally Begotten of the Father, God from God, Light from Light,
true God from true God, begotten, not made, of one Being with
the Father.

Through Him all things were made.
For us and for our salvation He came down from heaven:
by the power of the Holy Spirit

---

[1]*Refers to the universal Christian Church.*

He became incarnate from the Virgin Mary, and was made man.
For our sake He was crucified under Pontius Pilate;
He suffered death and was buried.
On the third day He rose again in accordance with the Scriptures;
He ascended into heaven and is seated
at the right hand of the Father.
He will come again in glory to judge the living and the dead,
and His kingdom will have no end.

We believe in the Holy Spirit, the Lord, the giver of life,
who proceeds from the Father and the Son.
With the Father and the Son He is worshipped and glorified.
He has spoken through the Prophets.

We believe in one holy catholic[2] and apostolic Church.
We acknowledge one baptism for the forgiveness of sins.
We look for the resurrection of the dead,
and the life of the world to come. Amen.

Athanasian Creed

Whosoever will be saved, before all things it is necessary that he
hold the catholic[3] faith, which faith except everyone do keep
whole and undefiled, without doubt he shall perish everlastingly.

And the catholic faith is this, that we worship one God in Trinity and
Trinity in Unity. Neither confounding the Persons, nor dividing
the Substance. For there is one Person of the Father, another of
the Son, and another of the Holy Ghost. But the Godhead of the
Father, of the Son and of the Holy Ghost is all One, the Glory
Equal, the Majesty Co-Eternal. Such as the Father is, such is the
Son, and such is the Holy Ghost. The Father Uncreate, the Son
Uncreate, and the Holy Ghost Uncreate. The Father
Incomprehensible, the Son Incomprehensible, and the Holy
Ghost Incomprehensible. The Father Eternal, the Son Eternal,
and the Holy Ghost Eternal and yet they are not Three Eternals

---

[2]*Refers to the universal Church.*
[3] *Refers to the universal Christian faith.*

but One Eternal. As also there are not Three Uncreated, nor Three Incomprehensibles, but One Uncreated, and One Uncomprehensible. So likewise the Father is Almighty, the Son Almighty, and the Holy Ghost Almighty.
And yet they are not Three Almighties but One Almighty.

So the Father is God, the Son is God, and the Holy Ghost is God. And yet they are not Three Gods, but One God. So likewise the Father is Lord, the Son Lord, and the Holy Ghost Lord. And yet not Three Lords but One Lord. For, like as we are compelled by the Christian verity to acknowledge every Person by Himself to be God and Lord, so are we forbidden by the catholic Religion to say, there be Three Gods or Three Lords. The Father is made of none, neither created, nor begotten. The Son is of the Father alone; not made, nor created, but begotten. The Holy Ghost is of the Father, and of the Son neither made, nor created, nor begotten, but proceeding.

So there is One Father, not Three Fathers; one Son, not Three Sons; One Holy Ghost, not Three Holy Ghosts. And in this Trinity none is afore or after other, none is greater or less than another, but the whole Three Persons are Co-eternal together, and Co-equal. So that in all things, as is aforesaid, the Unity in Trinity, and the Trinity in Unity, is to be worshipped. He therefore that will be saved, must thus think of the Trinity.

Furthermore, it is necessary to everlasting Salvation, that he also believe rightly the Incarnation of our Lord Jesus Christ. For the right Faith is, that we believe and confess, that Lord Jesus Christ, the Son of God, is God and Man.

God, of the substance of the Father, begotten before the worlds; and Man, of the substance of His mother, born into the world. Perfect God and Perfect Man, of a reasonable Soul and human Flesh subsisting. Equal to the Father as touching His Godhead, and inferior to the Father as touching His Manhood. Who, although He be God and Man, yet He is not two, but One Christ.

One, not by conversion of the Godhead into Flesh, but by taking of the Manhood into God. One altogether, not by confusion of substance, but by Unity of Person.

For as the reasonable soul and flesh is one Man, so God and Man is one Christ. Who suffered for our salvation, descended into hell, rose again the third day from the dead. He ascended into heaven, He sitteth on the right hand of the Father, God Almighty, from whence He shall come to judge the quick and the dead. At whose coming all men shall rise again with their bodies, and shall give account for their own works. And they that have done good shall go into life everlasting, and they that have done evil into everlasting fire.

This is the catholic faith[4], which except a man believe faithfully and firmly, he cannot be saved.

---

[4]*Refers to the universal Christian faith.*

Hymns in this guide (full text)

Sunday – Trinity

<u>Joyful, Joyful We Adore Thee</u> *(Words: Henry Van Dyke, 1907.)*

1. Joyful, joyful, we adore Thee,
God of glory, Lord of love;
Hearts unfold like flow'rs before Thee,
Op'ning to the sun above.
Melt the clouds of sin and sadness;
Drive the dark of doubt away;
Giver of immortal gladness,
Fill us with the light of day!

2. All Thy works with joy surround Thee,
Earth and heav'n reflect Thy rays,
Stars and angels sing around Thee,
Center of unbroken praise.
Field and forest, vale and mountain,
Flow'ry meadow, flashing sea,
Singing bird and flowing fountain
Call us to rejoice in Thee.

3. Thou art giving and forgiving,
Ever blessing, ever blest,
Wellspring of the joy of living,
Ocean depth of happy rest!
Thou our Father, Christ our Brother,
All who live in love are Thine;
Teach us how to love each other,
Lift us to the joy divine.

4. Mortals, join the happy chorus,
Which the morning stars began;
Father love is reigning o'er us,
Brother love binds man to man.
Ever singing, march we onward,
Victors in the midst of strife,

Joyful music leads us Sunward
In the triumph song of life.

<u>May the Grace of Christ our Savior</u> *(Words: John Newton, 1779.)*

1. May the grace of Christ our Savior
And the Father's boundless love
With the Holy Spirit's favor,
Rest upon us from above.

2. Thus may we abide in union
With each other and the Lord,
And possess, in sweet communion,
Joys which earth cannot afford.

<u>Holy, Holy, Holy</u> *(Words: Reginald Heber, 1826.)*

1. Holy, holy, holy! Lord God Almighty!
Early in the morning our song shall rise to Thee.
Holy, holy, holy! Merciful and mighty,
God in three Persons, blessed Trinity!

2. Holy, holy, holy! All the saints adore Thee,
Casting down their golden crowns around the glassy sea;
Cherubim and seraphim falling down before Thee,
Which wert, and art, and evermore shalt be.

3. Holy, holy, holy! Though the darkness hide Thee,
Though the eye of sinful man Thy glory may not see,
Only Thou art holy; there is none beside Thee,
Perfect in power, in love and purity.

4. Holy, holy, holy! Lord God Almighty!
All Thy works shall praise Thy name, in earth and sky and sea.
Holy, holy, holy! Merciful and mighty,
God in three Persons, blessed Trinity.

Monday – Resting

<u>For the Beauty of the Earth</u> *(Words: Folliot Pierpoint, 1864.)*

1. For the beauty of the earth
For the glory of the skies,
For the love which from our birth
Over and around us lies.

Refrain
Lord of all, to Thee we raise,
This our hymn of grateful praise.

2. For the beauty of each hour,
Of the day and of the night,
Hill and vale, and tree and flower,
Sun and moon, and stars of light.
Refrain

3. For the joy of ear and eye,
For the heart and mind's delight,
For the mystic harmony
Linking sense to sound and sight.
Refrain

4. For the joy of human love,
Brother, sister, parent, child,
Friends on earth and friends above,
For all gentle thoughts and mild.
Refrain

5. For Thy Church, that evermore
Lifteth holy hands above,
Offering up on every shore
Her pure sacrifice of love.
Refrain

6. For the martyrs' crown of light,
For Thy prophets' eagle eye,
For Thy bold confessors' might,
For the lips of infancy.
Refrain

7. For each perfect gift of Thine,
To our race so freely given,
Graces human and divine,
Flowers of earth and buds of Heaven.
Refrain

Tuesday – God Almighty

<u>Praise to the Lord, the Almighty</u> (*Words: Joachim Neander, 1680.*)

1. Praise to the Lord, the Almighty, the King of creation!
O my soul, praise Him, for He is thy health and salvation!
All ye who hear, now to His temple draw near;
Praise Him in glad adoration.

2. Praise to the Lord, Who over all things so wondrously reigneth,
Shelters thee under His wings, yea, so gently sustaineth!
Hast thou not seen how thy desires ever have been
Granted in what He ordaineth?

3. Praise to the Lord, Who hath fearfully, wondrously, made thee;
Health hath vouchsafed and, when heedlessly falling, hath stayed thee.
What need or grief ever hath failed of relief?
Wings of His mercy did shade thee.

4. Praise to the Lord, Who doth prosper thy work and defend thee;
Surely His goodness and mercy here daily attend thee.
Ponder anew what the Almighty can do,
If with His love He befriend thee.

5. Praise to the Lord, Who, when tempests their warfare are waging,
Who, when the elements madly around thee are raging,
Biddeth them cease, turneth their fury to peace,
Whirlwinds and waters assuaging.

6. Praise to the Lord, Who, when darkness of sin is abounding,
Who, when the godless do triumph, all virtue confounding,
Sheddeth His light, chaseth the horrors of night,
Saints with His mercy surrounding.

7. Praise to the Lord, O let all that is in me adore Him!
All that hath life and breath, come now with praises before Him.
Let the Amen sound from His people again,
Gladly for aye we adore Him.

Wednesday – Longing

<u>Jesus, the Joy of Loving Hearts</u> *(Words: Bernard of Clairvaux, 12th Century; translated: Ray Palmer, 1858.)*

1. Jesus the Joy of loving hearts
Our Fount of Life, the Light of men
From the best bliss that earth imparts
We turn unfilled to You again.

2. Your truth unchanging ever stood
You save us when to You we call
To those who seek You, You are good
To those who find in You all in all.

3. We taste You, oh our living Bread
And long to feed upon You still
We drink from You, our Source, our Head
And thirst our souls from You to fill.

4. Our restless spirits yearn for You
Whatever lot or change may be
Glad when Your gracious smile we see
Bless'd when by faith we can cling to You.

5. O, Jesus, ever with us stay
Help our souls find You in the night
You make our moments bright as day
Shed o'er the world Your holy light.

<u>Come, Thou Fount</u> *(Words: Robert Robinson, 1758.)*

1. Come, Thou Fount of every blessing,
Tune my heart to sing Thy grace;
Streams of mercy, never ceasing,
Call for songs of loudest praise.
Teach me some melodious sonnet,
Sung by flaming tongues above.

Praise the Fount! I'm fixed upon it,
Fount of Thy redeeming love.

2. Here I raise my Ebenezer;
Here by Thy great help I've come;
And I hope, by Thy good pleasure,
Safely to arrive at home.
Jesus sought me when a stranger,
Wandering from the fold of God;
He, to rescue me from danger,
Interposed His precious blood.

3. O to grace how great a debtor
Daily I'm constrained to be!
Let Thy goodness, like a fetter,
Bind my wandering heart to Thee.
Prone to wander, Lord, I feel it,
Prone to leave the God I love;
Here's my heart, O take and seal it,
Seal it for Thy courts above.

4. O that day when freed from sinning,
I shall see Thy lovely face;
Clothed then in blood washed linen
How I'll sing Thy sovereign grace;
Come, my Lord, no longer tarry,
Take my ransomed soul away;
Send Thine angels now to carry
Me to realms of endless day.

Thursday – Jesus Christ

<u>Be Thou My Vision</u> *(Words: tr. Mary Byrne, 1905.)*

1. Be Thou my Vision, O Lord of my heart
Naught be all else to me save that Thou art
Thou my best thought by day or by night
Waking or sleeping Thy presence my light.

2. Be Thou my Wisdom, and Thou my true Word
I ever with Thee and Thou with me, Lord
Thou my great Father, I Thy true son
Thou in me dwelling and I with Thee one.

3. Be Thou my breastplate, my sword for the fight
Be Thou my whole armor, be Thou my true might
Be Thou my soul's shelter, be Thou my strong tower
O, raise Thou me heav'nward, great Power of my power.

4. Riches I heed not nor man's empty praise
Thou mine inheritance now and always
Thou and Thou only first in my heart
High King of heaven my Treasure Thou art.

5. High King of heaven when victory's won
May I reach heavn's joys, O bright heaven's Sun
Heart of my own heart whatever befall
Still be my Vision, O Ruler of all.

O Come, O Come, Emmanuel (*Words: tr. John M. Neale, 1851.*)

1. O come, O come, Emmanuel,
And ransom captive Israel,
That mourns in lonely exile here
Until the Son of God appear.

Refrain
Rejoice! Rejoice! Emmanuel.
Shall come to thee, O Israel.

2. O come, Thou Wisdom from on high,
Who orderest all things mightily;
To us the path of knowledge show,
And teach us in her ways to go.
Refrain

3. O come, Thou Rod of Jesse,
Free Thine own from Satan's tyranny;
From depths of hell Thy people save,
And give them victory over the grave.
Refrain

4. O come, Thou Day-spring, come and cheer
Our spirits by Thine advent here;
Disperse the gloomy clouds of night,
And death's dark shadows put to flight.
Refrain

5. O come, Thou Key of David, come,
And open wide our heavenly home;
Make safe the way that leads on high,
And close the path to misery.
Refrain

6. O come, O come, great Lord of might,
Who to Thy tribes on Sinai's height
In ancient times once gave the law
In cloud and majesty and awe.
Refrain

7. O come, Thou Root of Jesse's tree,
An ensign of Thy people be;
Before Thee rulers silent fall;
All peoples on Thy mercy call.
Refrain

8. O come, Desire of Nations, bind
In one the hearts of all mankind;
Bid Thou our sad divisions cease,
And be Thyself our King of Peace.
Refrain

Friday – Abiding

<u>May the Mind of Christ, My Savior</u> *(Words: Kate Wilkinson, 1925.)*

1. May the mind of Christ, my Savior,
Live in me from day to day,
By His love and power controlling
All I do and say.

2. May the Word of God dwell richly
In my heart from hour to hour,
So that all may see I triumph
Only through His power.

3. May the peace of God my Father
Rule my life in everything,
That I may be calm to comfort
Sick and sorrowing.

4. May the love of Jesus fill me
As the waters fill the sea;
Him exalting, self abasing,
This is victory.

5. May I run the race before me,
Strong and brave to face the foe,
Looking only unto Jesus
As I onward go.

6. May His beauty rest upon me,
As I seek the lost to win,
And may they forget the channel,
Seeing only Him.

Saturday – Holy Spirit

Spirit Divine *(Words: Andrew Reed, 1829.)*

1. Spirit divine, attend our prayer,
And make our heart Thy home;
Descend with all Thy gracious power;
Come, Holy Spirit, come.

2. Come as the light, to us reveal
The truth we long to know;
Reveal the narrow path of right,
The way of duty show.

3. Come as the fire and purge our hearts
Like sacrificial flame,
Till our whole souls an offering be
In Love's redeeming name.

4. Come as the dew, and sweetly bless
This consecrated hour;
May barrenness rejoice to own
Thy fertilizing power.

5. Come as the dove, and spread Thy wings,
The wings of peaceful love;
And let Thy Church on earth become
Blest as Thy Church above.

6. Come as the wind, O Breath of God!
O Pentecostal grace!
Come, make Thy great salvation known,
Wide as the human race.

7. Spirit divine, attend our prayer;
Make a lost world Thy home;
Descend with all Thy gracious powers,
O come, great Spirit, come.

Other Recommended Reading

1. Adam, David. 2nd ed. (2007). *The Rhythm of Life*. Morehouse Publishing, New York, NY.

2. Baab, L. M. (2005). *Sabbath Keeping*. InterVarsity Press, Downers Grove, IL.

3. Calhoun, A. A. (2005). *Spiritual Disciplines Handbook*. InterVarsity Press, Downers Grove, IL.

4. Foster, R. J. & Smith, J. B. (rev. 2005). *Devotional Classics*. Harper Collins, New York, NY.

5. The Northumbria Community (2002). *Celtic Daily Prayer*. Harper Collins, New York, NY.

6. The Episcopal Church (1979). *Book of Common Prayer*. Church Publishing Incorporated.

7. Willard, D. (1991). *The Spirit of the Disciplines*. Harper Collins, New York, NY.

7

Notes and Sources

Scripture verses are taken from the King James Version unless otherwise stated. Unless annotated, prose, prayers, and other texts have been adapted or written by the author.

2. What is a "Daily Office"?

Adam, David, The Rhythm of Life-Celtic Daily Prayer, p. 6.
**Gloria Patri is also known as the minor doxology. This refers to the traditional prayer "Glory to the Father, and to the Son, and to the Holy Spirit. As it was in the beginning, is now, and ever shall be, world without end. Amen."*

Sunday - Trinity

Benediction – Adapted from 2 Corinthians 13: 14.
**Afternoon Affirmation – Text from hymn "May the Grace of Christ our Savior".*

Monday - Resting

* Morning Prayer – Psalm 23 (NKJV).*
**Afternoon prayer – Doxology.*
***Evening Benediction – Adapted portion of St. Patrick's Breast-plate.*

Tuesday - God Almighty

Morning Affirmation – Deuteronomy 6: 4-5.
**Morning Prayer* – The Lord's or Disciple's Prayer in Matthew 6: 9-13.

Wednesday - Longing

Morning Prayer – Adapted from Psalm 27: 4.

Thursday - Jesus Christ

Morning Acclamation – Adapted from a traditional Celtic prayer attributed to St. Patrick.

Friday - Abiding

Benediction – Gloria Patri.

Saturday - Holy Spirit

Morning Prayer – Adapted from Hannah's prayer in 1 Samuel 2: 1-10.
**Benediction* – Adapted from Psalm 121.

Notes